VIBES ACROSS THE DIASPORA

VOLUME 1

DONOVAN TINSLEY

Copyright © 2025 by Donovan Tinsley

All rights reserved.

No part of this book may be reproduced, stored in a retrieval system, or transmitted in any form or by any means, electronic, mechanical, photocopying, recording, or otherwise, without the prior written permission of the author, except as provided by USA copyright law.

Food Photographer: Donovan Tinsley

Graphic Designer: Kerlie Mérizier (KM Designs)

Hardcover Book ISBN: 979-8-9933775-0-6

Printed in the United States of America

T. Fielding-Lowe Company, Publisher

https://www.tfieldinglowecompany.com

DEDICATION

This cookbook is dedicated to my village, those who have been there for me across the many stages of my life.

First, I give honor to God for blessing me with my gifts and guiding my steps as I continue unfolding the plan He has in store for me.

To my ancestors, thank you for your sacrifices and for paving the way, allowing me to live out your wildest dreams.

To my parents, who opened my eyes to cooking, diverse cuisines, and nurtured my craft, humor, and character.

To my sister, my biggest supporter and lifelong cheerleader.

To my grandmother, the elders in my family, and my church community, thank you for your prayers and for speaking words of encouragement and protection over my life.

To my extended family and closest friends, thank you for being my taste testers, thought partners, and motivators.

And to the Soul de Alma supporters, and everyone in between, thank you for helping me build a virtual community where I can share my love for food, life, and history beyond the bounds of my village.

Thank you all for seeing the vision before I could. Cheers to this being the first of many great things to come from Soul de Alma.

I love y'all.

Table of
CONTENTS

9   About Soul de Alma

10   Permission to Explore

11   Pre Prep/ Prep/ Cook

12   Commonly Used Seasonings

13   Freedom to Substitute

14   Cleaning Meat

15   **Beans**
Black Beans
Black-Eyed Peas
Habichuela Guisada

18   **Beef**
Beef Stew
Chili

22   **Chicken**
Curry Chicken
Fried Chicken
Haitian Fried Chicken

27   **Drinks**
Coquito
Morir Soñando
Rum Swizzle

31   **Empanadas**
Beef
Chicken
Tuna

Marinades 37
Epis
Green Seasoning
Sofrito

Pasta 40
Mac & Cheese
Macaroni Salad
Lasagna
Spaghetti

Pork 45
Chuletas
Pernil

Rice 48
Arroz con Gandules
Red Rice
Rice and Peas

Sides 52
Dominican Potato Salad
Mayoketchup
Pastelón
Red Onions
Yams

Soup 58
Caldeirada de Cabrito
Chicken Noodle Soup
Sancocho

Sweets 64
Banana Bread
Pudin de Pan
Sweet Potato Pie

Vegetables 68
Cabbage
Collard Greens
Shucked Corn

Index 74
References 75
About Donovan 78

ABOUT SOUL DE ALMA

Welcome to an inclusive space where soul food from across the African diaspora awaits you.

This platform was born from Donovan's deep passion for cooking and his ongoing journey of healing, learning, and embracing what it truly means to be "Black". Throughout history, anti-Blackness has taken many forms. But here, we highlight the richness, resilience, and complexity of our identities, beyond pain—through food, exploration, and humor.

Throughout this journey, Donovan highlights, celebrates, and pays homage to dishes from across the diaspora while igniting a sense of nostalgia and belonging. Irrespective of your ethnic background, his mission is to share the transformative process of falling in love with yourself and your culture.

Through this platform, we hope to build a community that inspires each of us to dream boldly and show up as our most authentic selves, unapologetically.

Let this serve as a reminder: life is too short, random, and beautiful to stay stuck in your thoughts.

Soul de Alma is proof of what is possible when we stop letting fear of the unknown or failure hold us back.

PERMISSION TO EXPLORE

Cooking is a powerful way to express and showcase your creativity. Many of the recipes in this cookbook come from years of "eyeballing" ingredients, guided by instinct, not measurements. I relied entirely on the wisdom of the ancestors while assessing each dish by color, texture, and taste. It wasn't until I began this project that I considered measuring ingredients, so that the final result would taste as if I made it for you in my own kitchen.

I give you full permission to explore and experiment with the dishes in this book.

Let the ingredients and measurements serve as a starting point. If you feel like adding more of something, do it. If a seasoning doesn't speak to you, skip it. If you're a "tarian" (vegetarian, pescatarian, or have dietary restrictions), feel free to substitute the meat with your preferred protein or plant-based option.

Think it might taste better with your own twist? Baby, add it, and put us on! Have fun, trust your instincts, and cook with love.

May your exploration and creativity inspire you to create even tastier versions of what's in this book.

PRE-PREP/PREP/COOK

Cooking is a labor of love. Some dishes in this book may come together in under 30 minutes, while others may take a few hours to prepare. This page is designed to help you plan and organize your process, so cooking feels less stressful and more enjoyable.

Pre-Prep:
- ☐ Clean and declutter your kitchen
- ☐ Create a shopping list, double-checking that you have every ingredient for your meal
- ☐ Unpack and store ingredients/groceries
- ☐ Clean and store meat correctly
    - ☐ Sanitize all surfaces that came into contact with raw meat
- ☐ Prepare your marinades (See pages 37-39)
- ☐ Thaw frozen meat

Prep:
- ☐ Put on your favorite playlist or podcast
- ☐ Layout your ingredients and cookware
- ☐ Season and marinate the meat
- ☐ Chop the vegetables

Cook:
- ☐ Review the recipe instructions
- ☐ Clean as you cook
- ☐ Monitor your food as it cooks
- ☐ Taste and adjust the flavor to your liking
- ☐ Serve and enjoy your food
- ☐ Pack and properly store leftovers

COMMONLY USED SEASONINGS

The following ingredients will appear in recipes throughout this cookbook. Use this page to ensure you have everything before making your meal.

Herbs
Oregano
Garlic Powder
Parsley
Ginger Powder
Onion Powder
Paprika
Thyme
Soy Dominicano Oregano

Spices
Black Pepper
Cinnamon
Nutmeg
Allspice
Cloves

Oil
Vegetable Oil
Olive Oil

Special Seasonings
Adobo
Old Bay Seasoning
Lawry's Seasoned Salt
Sazón
Badia Sazón Completa
Blue Mountain Curry Powder
Blue Mountain Ginger Allspice Escallion Mix
Chicken Bouillon
Kreyol Heritage Koupe Dwet All-Purpose Seasoning

Liquid Seasonings
Badia Naranja Agria
Badia Mojo
Ranchero Salsa Inglesa
Vinegar

Other
Salt
Sugar
Vanilla
Brown Sugar
Pam Baking Spray

FREEDOM TO SUBSTITUTE

This book has been curated based on my preferences, but remember that cooking comes from the heart. If you wish to substitute ingredients in these recipes, I have created a list of alternatives to whatever your preference is. Have fun!

Meat
Chicken
Turkey
Beef
Pork
Fish varieties

Vegetables
Fresh
Canned
Frozen

Dairy/Lactose
Lactose-free milk
Coconut milk
Almond milk
Soy milk
Cashew milk

Oils
Vegetable oil
Avocado oil
Extra virgin olive oil
Canola oil
Corn oil
Sunflower oil
Achiote oil

Rice
White rice (grain-length varieties)
Brown rice
Jasmine rice
Parboiled rice
Basmati rice

Stock/Broth
Chicken
Vegetable
Turkey
Beef
Bone
Fish

Specific Substitutions in this Cookbook
1 2-inch chunk of ginger > *½ teaspoon of ground ginger*
5 allspice berries > *⅛ teaspoon of ground allspice*
10 allspice berries > *¼ teaspoon of ground allspice*
1 teaspoon of dried Badia Mojo seasoning > *1 tablespoon of Badia Mojo Marinade*
1 packet of chicken bouillon > *2 tablespoons of chicken bouillon*
Scotch bonnet pepper > *habanero pepper*
Aji dulce > *sweet bell peppers*
Calabaza pumpkin > *butternut squash*
culantro > *cilantro*

CLEANING MEAT

For centuries, across the African diaspora and beyond, the practice of cleaning meat before seasoning and cooking it has been a significant cultural tradition. This process, deeply rooted in our history, rids the meat of any potential germs and impurities, ensuring it's safe to eat. The tradition is closely tied to the experiences of enslaved people and their descendants, who often received animal scraps and less desirable cuts. These parts required careful, thorough washing before cooking. A good example of this, chitlins, a southern delicacy made from pig intestines.

This step is more than just food safety; it's an enhancement to flavor. Many of the dishes in this book benefit from this process. Below are the recommended steps for cleaning raw meat and sanitizing your kitchen afterward.

How to clean meat:

Step 1: Remove any excess skin or fat
Step 2: Pour vinegar, squeeze, and scrub lime into the meat
Step 3: Soak the meat in vinegar, lime juice, and cold water for 5 to 15 minutes
Step 4: (optional) Soak and rinse the meat in hot water
Step 5: Drain the meat of any excess water before seasoning

How to clean your space after cleaning meat:

Step 1: Spray all surfaces and cookware that came into contact with raw meat using an all-purpose or bleach-based disinfectant
Step 2: Rinse with hot water
Step 3: Wash dishes and surfaces with dish soap
Step 4: Rinse again and dry completely

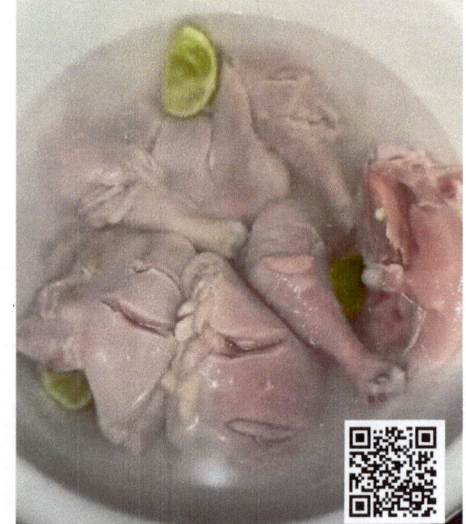

Check out the beginning of this video for a demonstration

Black Beans

INGREDIENTS

- 1 15 oz can of black beans
- ½ cup of water
- 2 tablespoons of sofrito
- 2 teaspoons of garlic powder
- 1 teaspoon of Badia Sazón Completo
- 1 packet of Sazón
- ¾ teaspoon of Adobo
- ½ teaspoon of paprika
- ½ teaspoon of Soy Dominicano Oregano
- ½ teaspoon of parsley
- 1 tablespoon of olive oil
- 1 clove of garlic, minced

PRE-PREP

1. Prepare the sofrito (see page 39).

COOK

1. Sauté the sofrito and garlic in 1 tablespoon of olive oil.
2. Open the can of beans and add the contents, including the liquid.
3. Stir in the water and seasonings.
4. Reduce the heat and let the beans simmer for 15–20 minutes.

Fun Fact

Black beans are native to the Americas and have been a staple in diets across the continents for more than 7,000 years.[1]

Black-Eyed Peas

INGREDIENTS

- 1 16 oz bag of black-eyed peas
- 1 lb of smoked turkey necks
- 1 medium yellow onion
- 1 medium green bell pepper
- 1 medium red bell pepper
- 2 sticks of celery
- 3 garlic cloves, chopped
- 3 bay leaves
- 2½ teaspoons of paprika
- 2½ teaspoons of garlic powder
- 2½ teaspoons of onion powder
- 1 teaspoon of black pepper
- 2½ teaspoons of Lawry's Seasoned Salt
- 1 packet of chicken bouillon
- 1 teaspoon of vinegar
- 1 tablespoon of olive oil

PRE-PREP

1. Chop the vegetables.
2. Boil the turkey necks in water for 1 hour.
3. Sort the peas.
   Tip: Peas should be smooth and free from any signs of damage. If a pea appears discolored, broken, moldy, or shriveled, discard it.
4. Rinse and soak the peas overnight, or for at least 6 hours.

COOK

1. Sauté the chopped vegetables in the olive oil. Add the pre-boiled smoked meat and water.
   Tip: Add enough water to cover the meat completely.
2. Lightly season the water and turkey necks.
3. Once the water reaches a boil, add the peas along with the water in which you soaked them.
4. Add the remaining seasoning to the beans.
5. Cook the peas over low to medium heat for 1½ to 2 hours.
   a. The turkey necks should be falling off the bone about 1 hour into cooking. If they are not, remove them and shred them with a fork.
   b. During this time, remove and mash a few of the peas to help thicken the broth.
   c. Taste the broth and adjust the seasoning as needed.
6. Cook on low for the final 30 minutes.

Fun Fact

Every New Year, many Black Americans prepare this dish to welcome luck and good fortune in the year ahead.

Habichuela Guisada

INGREDIENTS

- 2 15 oz cans of pink beans
- 1 medium red onion
- 1 medium green bell pepper
- 2 cloves of garlic
- 4 tablespoons of sofrito
- 2 cups of 1-inch chunks of calabaza pumpkin
- ½ teaspoon of black pepper
- ½ teaspoon of dried oregano
- ½ teaspoon of Soy Dominicano Oregano
- ½ teaspoon of thyme
- ½ teaspoon of dried parsley
- 1 tablespoon of Badia Sazón Completa
- 1 teaspoon of Adobo
- 1 teaspoon of vinegar
- 1 tablespoon of garlic powder
- ½ cup of water
- 1 packet of chicken bouillon
- ¼ bunch of fresh cilantro
- 1 tablespoon of olive oil

PRE-PREP

1. Make the sofrito (see page 39).

PREP

1. Peel the calabaza and cut it into 1-inch chunks.
2. Chop the vegetables.
3. Add 1 can of beans and its juices, along with a few pieces of calabaza, green pepper, onion, 2 tablespoons of sofrito, and water to a blender.
4. Drain and rinse the other can of pink beans.

COOK

1. Sauté the onions, peppers, and garlic in olive oil.
2. Add 2 tablespoons of sofrito.
3. Incorporate the drained beans.
4. Stir in the blended bean mixture.
5. Season the beans. Once the beans reach a boil, add fresh cilantro, reduce the heat, and cook for another 10-15 minutes.
6. During this time, taste the beans and adjust the seasoning as needed.

Fun Fact

Stewing is the most common method of preparing beans in the Caribbean and Latin America.[2]

Beef Stew 🇩🇴

INGREDIENTS

- 2 ½ lbs. of cubed stew beef
- 1 medium yellow onion
- 1 medium red onion
- 1 medium green bell pepper
- 1 medium red bell pepper
- 3 cloves of garlic, minced
- ½ a can (approx. 3 oz) of tomato paste
- 1 packet of Sazón
- 1 cup of sofrito
- 1 teaspoon of black pepper
- 2 ½ teaspoons of Adobo
- 3 teaspoons of Badia Sazón Completa
- 3 teaspoons of garlic powder
- 1 teaspoon of oregano
- 1 teaspoon of Soy Dominicano Oregano
- 1 teaspoon of paprika
- 1 teaspoon of onion powder
- 1 teaspoon of thyme
- 1 teaspoon of parsley
- 1 teaspoon of Ranchero Salsa Inglesa
- 1 tablespoon of Badia Naranja Agria
- 2 bay leaves
- Squeeze of lime juice
- 1 ½ tablespoons of olive oil
- 1 tablespoon of brown sugar
- 1 capful of vinegar

PRE-PREP

1. Make the sofrito (see page 39).

PREP

1. Chop the vegetables.
2. Clean the beef:
    a. Remove any excess fat.
    b. Soak in cold water with lime and vinegar.

3. Season and marinate the beef for at least 30 minutes.
   - Below are the measurements for the marinade:
     - 1 packet of Sazón
     - ½ teaspoon of black pepper
     - 1 teaspoon of Adobo
     - 1 teaspoon of Badia Sazón Completa
     - 2 teaspoons of garlic powder
     - ½ teaspoon of oregano
     - ½ teaspoon of Soy Dominicano Oregano
     - ½ teaspoon of paprika
     - ½ teaspoon of onion powder
     - ½ teaspoon of thyme
     - ½ teaspoon of parsley
     - 3 tablespoons of sofrito
     - 1 tablespoon of Badia Naranja Agria
     - 1 teaspoon of Ranchero Salsa Inglesa
     - Squeeze of lime juice
4. After seasoning the beef, add the chopped vegetables and marinate them together.

COOK

1. Optional: On low heat, combine the oil and brown sugar in a pot.
2. Add the marinated beef and sear for several minutes.
3. Stir in the sofrito and tomato paste, then season.
4. Add water, bay leaves, and vinegar.
5. Simmer on low heat for 1½ hours, or until the beef is tender.
   Tip #1: Check the stew every 7–10 minutes and add water as needed.
   Tip #2: Around the 60-minute mark, taste and adjust the seasoning to your preference.

Fun Fact

This dish appears in many forms around the world, with roots reaching back to 14th-century France, and an even older history beyond that.[3]

Chili

INGREDIENTS

- 3 lbs. of ground beef
- 1 cup of sofrito
- 1 medium yellow onion
- 1 medium red onion
- 1 medium green bell pepper
- 1 medium red bell pepper
- ¼ bunch of fresh cilantro
- ¼ bunch of fresh culantro
- 4 cloves of garlic, minced or chopped
- 1 28 oz can of diced tomatoes
- 1 15 oz can of black beans
- 1 15 oz can of red beans
- 1 16 oz can of corn (optional)
- 2 ½ tablespoons of Adobo
- 2 packets of Sazón
- 2 ½ tablespoons of Lawry's Seasoned Salt
- 1 ½ tablespoons of Badia Sazón Completa
- 1 teaspoon of black pepper
- 1 teaspoon of paprika
- 1 tablespoon of garlic powder
- 2 teaspoons of onion powder
- 1 teaspoon of oregano
- 1 teaspoon of parsley
- 1 teaspoon of thyme
- 1 teaspoon of hot sauce
- 2 tablespoons of sugar or syrup
- 29 oz of tomato sauce (1 ½ cans)

PRE-PREP

1. Make the sofrito (see page 39).

PREP

1. Chop the vegetables.
2. Drain the juice from the diced tomatoes.
3. Partially cook the ground beef, lightly seasoning it, and add ⅓ cup of sofrito to render some fat.
4. Drain the beef, reserving 1-2 tablespoons of the fat in the pot.
5. Set the cooked beef aside.

Chili (Cont.)

COOK

1. Sauté the vegetables with ⅓ cup of sofrito over medium heat.
2. Once softened, add the beans and tomatoes, then season.
3. Return the ground beef to the pot and season again.
4. Stir in the tomato sauce and additional sofrito, followed by a few dashes of hot sauce and either sugar or maple syrup.
5. Reduce the heat and let simmer for 10 to 20 minutes.
6. Taste the chili and adjust the seasoning to your preference.
7. Stir in freshly chopped cilantro and culantro, then allow the dish to cool slightly before serving.

Fun Fact

Chili is best enjoyed with a side of white rice, cornbread, or both.

Curry Chicken

INGREDIENTS

- 5 chicken thighs
- 5 chicken drumsticks
- 2 teaspoons of Blue Mountain Allspice, Garlic, and Escallion Seasoning
- 2 teaspoons of Blue Mountain Curry Powder
- 2 teaspoons of Grace or Badia Curry Powder
- ½ teaspoon of black pepper
- 2 ½ teaspoons of garlic powder
- ½ teaspoon of onion powder
- ½ teaspoon of paprika
- ½ teaspoon of dried thyme
- 2 tablespoons of green seasoning
- ½ teaspoon of dried oregano
- 1 teaspoon of ginger powder
- ½ teaspoon of parsley
- 1 packet of chicken bouillon
- 1 ½ tablespoons of olive oil
- 2 medium carrots, peeled
- 3 medium yellow potatoes
- 1 medium green bell pepper
- 1 medium yellow onion
- 3 stems of fresh thyme
- ½ cup of chopped scallions
- 5 allspice berries

PRE-PREP

1. Make the green seasoning (see page 38).

PREP

1. Prep the chicken by removing the skin.
2. Clean the chicken by soaking and scrubbing it in a mixture of water, lime, and vinegar.
3. Season and marinate for at least one hour.
4. Chop the vegetables into ½ inch chunks and the potatoes into 1-inch chunks.

COOK

1. Burn the curry by combining oil and curry powder over medium heat until the mixture darkens in color.
2. Add the chicken, cover the pot, and cook for 15 minutes over medium-low heat.
3. Add 2-3 cups of water to the marinade bowl for later use.
4. At the 15-minute mark, check the chicken. Depending on how much liquid it releases, add 1½–2 cups of the reserved marinade water.
   Tip: Do not fully cover the chicken with water.
5. Add additional seasoning, green seasoning, and the vegetables. Cover and cook for another 15 minutes.

Curry Chicken (Cont.)

6. After 10 minutes, reduce the heat to low and place the potatoes on top of the chicken. Cover again.
   Tip: Do not stir the potatoes in too early, or the gravy will become too thick.
7. Once the potatoes are fork-tender, remove from the heat and serve.

Fun Fact
Jamaican curry chicken reflects a rich blend of Indian, African, and English influences, and is best enjoyed with rice and steamed vegetables.

Fried Chicken

INGREDIENTS

- 3 lbs. of chicken (any cut is suitable)
- 1 teaspoon of black pepper
- 2 teaspoons of garlic powder
- 2 teaspoons of onion powder
- 1 teaspoon of thyme
- 1 teaspoon of oregano
- 1 teaspoon of parsley
- 1 teaspoon of Soy Dominicano Oregano
- 2½ teaspoons of Old Bay Seasoning
- 2 teaspoons of Lawry's Seasoned Salt
- 2 ½ cups of all-purpose flour
- 24 oz vegetable oil *

PREP

1. Clean the chicken with lime, vinegar and water.
2. Season and marinate the chicken for at least 30 minutes with the following:
   - ½ teaspoon of black pepper
   - 1 teaspoon of garlic powder
   - 1 teaspoon of onion powder
   - ½ teaspoon of thyme
   - ½ teaspoon of oregano
   - ½ teaspoon of parsley
   - ½ teaspoon of Soy Dominicano Oregano
   - 1 ½ teaspoons of Old Bay
   - 1 teaspoon of Lawry's Seasoned Salt
3. In a separate bowl, season all-purpose flour with:
   - ½ teaspoon of black pepper
   - 1 teaspoon of garlic powder
   - 1 teaspoon of onion powder
   - ½ teaspoon of thyme
   - ½ teaspoon of oregano
   - ½ teaspoon of parsley
   - ½ teaspoon of Soy Dominicano Oregano
   - 1 teaspoon of Old Bay Seasoning
   - 1 teaspoon of Lawry's Seasoned Salt

Scan or click here to watch video

*Depending on the size of the pot, you may not need to use this amount of oil. Use enough so there is about 2-3 inches of oil at the bottom of the pot..

Fried Chicken (Cont.)

COOK

1. Heat vegetable oil in a pot over medium heat.
2. While the oil heats, coat the chicken pieces in the seasoned flour, shaking off any excess.
3. Once the oil is hot, carefully add a few pieces of chicken to the pot.
4. Fry until golden brown and fully cooked, about 12 to 20 minutes depending on the size of the pieces.
   Tip: Bone-in chicken requires a longer cooking time.
5. The chicken is done when the juices run clear and the internal temperature reaches 165°F (74°C).
6. Remove the chicken from the pot and place it on a cooling rack or paper towels to drain excess oil.

Fun Fact

"If you look at the historical roots of entrepreneurship of people of African descent, since they became enslaved people, [fried chicken] was one of the few things that one could multiply and sell" - Frederick Douglass Opie[4]

Haitian Fried Chicken

INGREDIENTS

- 5 chicken thighs
- 5 chicken drumsticks
- 2 tablespoons of epis or ½ tablespoon of Kreyol Koupe Dwet Allspice Blend
- 1½ teaspoons of garlic powder
- 1 teaspoon of Badia Sazón Completa
- 1 teaspoon of Adobo
- ½ teaspoon of black pepper
- ½ teaspoon of paprika
- ½ teaspoon of oregano
- 1 teaspoon of chicken bouillon
- ½ teaspoon of Soy Dominicano Oregano
- ½ teaspoon of thyme
- 1 tablespoon of Badia Naranja Agria
- Squeeze of lime juice
- 3 cups of vegetable oil

PRE-PREP

1. Make the epis (see page 37).

PREP

1. Boil 1 qt of water to use for the final step of cleaning the chicken.
2. Prep the chicken by removing the skin and cutting medium to deep slits into the meat.
3. Clean the chicken by scrubbing and soaking it in a mixture of water, lime, and vinegar.
4. Rinse the chicken under the pre-boiled water.
5. Season and marinate the chicken for at least 1 hour.
6. Pour oil into a large pan and preheat it for 2-4 minutes before adding the partially cooked chicken from the pot.

COOK

1. Place the chicken in a pot and par-cook for 10-15 minutes, depending on the size of the pieces.
2. Remove the chicken from the pot, transfer to a plate, and let rest while the oil heats.
3. Once the oil is hot, carefully add the chicken and fry until golden brown on both sides.
4. Transfer the cooked chicken to a plate lined with paper towels to absorb excess oil before serving.

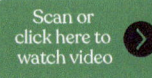 

Fun Fact

The term *Poul Fri* translates to 'fried chicken' in Haitian Creole and has roots in both West African and French culinary traditions.

Coquito

INGREDIENTS

- 1 12 oz can of evaporated milk
- 1 15 oz can of Coco López Crema de Coco
- 1 15 oz can of coconut milk
- 1 14 oz can of condensed milk
- 2 cups of Goslings Black Rum
- 1 16 oz can of coconut water with or without chunks
- ½ teaspoon of cinnamon
- ¼ teaspoon of nutmeg
- ¼ teaspoon of ground allspice
- ¼ teaspoon of ground clove
- 1 tablespoon of vanilla
- 1 2-inch chunk of fresh ginger
- 5 allspice berries
- 3 cloves
- 2 star anise pods or seeds

PREP

1. Peel the ginger.
2. Cook the coconut water with the whole spices and ginger.
    a. If you don't prefer coconut chunks in your Coquito, strain the coconut water as you pour it into the pot.
3. Bring to a boil, then turn off the heat.
4. Remove the spices and ginger, and let the coconut water cool.
5. In a large bowl, combine the canned milk, creams, and cooled coconut water. Mix or blend after each addition, starting with the thickest consistency:
    - Condensed milk
    - Crema de Coco
    - Coconut milk
    - Evaporated milk
    - Coconut water

   Tip: If the coconut water is still hot, do not add the rum. Let the mixture cool completely first.
6. Incorporate the spices and vanilla, then whisk or blend until smooth.
7. Stir in two or more cups of liquor and mix well. Refrigerate, serve chilled, and most importantly, drink responsibly.

   Tip: The longer the Coquito sits, the richer the flavor becomes.

DRINKS

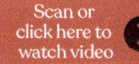 

Coquito (Cont.)

Lactose Intolerant Alternative:

Use only Crema de Coco, coconut milk, and coconut water. You can substitute the evaporated and condensed milk with lactose-free milk and condensed coconut milk. If using condensed coconut milk, add an extra ½ cup of evaporated milk to balance the sweetness.

Fun Fact

Coquito, which means 'little coconut' in Spanish, is traditionally prepared only during the holiday season.

Morir Soñando 🇩🇴

INGREDIENTS

- 18 oz of evaporated milk
- 1 14 oz can of condensed milk
- 3 ½ cups of orange juice
- 2 tablespoons of sugar
- 1 tablespoon of brown sugar
- 1 tablespoon of vanilla
- ⅛ teaspoon of ground cinnamon

ASSEMBLE

1. Combine the milk(s) and orange juice.
2. Add the sugar, vanilla, and cinnamon, then mix well.
   Tip: Taste at this stage and adjust the sweetness or seasoning to your preference.
3. Chill until ready to serve.

Fun Fact

Morir Soñando, which translates to 'to die dreaming,' originated in the Dominican Republic.

Rum Swizzle

INGREDIENTS

- 2¼ cups of orange juice
- 2 cups of pineapple juice
- 1 cup of Gosglings Black Seal Rum
- 1 cup of Bacardi's Spiced Rum
- ¼ cup of grenadine
- 1 lime, juiced
- 5 dashes of Angostura Bitters
- 2 maraschino cherries to garnish

ASSEMBLE

1. Mix the orange and pineapple juices together.
2. Add the grenadine, lime juice, rum, and bitters, then stir well.
   Tip: Taste at this stage and adjust the balance of flavors to your liking.
3. Chill until ready to serve.

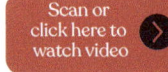

Fun Fact
The drink's name comes from the swizzle stick traditionally used to stir it, made from the Quararibea turbinata tree.[5]

Beef Empanadas

INGREDIENTS

- 2 pack of Goya empanada shells
- 3 lbs. of ground beef
- 1 cup of sofrito
- 1 medium yellow onion
- 1 medium red onion
- 1 medium green bell pepper
- 1 medium red bell pepper
- ¼ bunch of fresh cilantro
- ¼ bunch of fresh culantro
- 3 cloves of garlic, minced or chopped
- 2 medium plum tomatoes, diced
- 2 ½ tablespoons of Adobo
- 2 packets of Sazón
- 2 ½ tablespoons of Badia Sazón Completa
- 1 teaspoon of black pepper
- 1 teaspoon of paprika
- 1 tablespoon of garlic powder
- 2 teaspoons of onion powder
- 1 teaspoon of oregano
- 1 teaspoon of parsley
- 1 teaspoon of Soy Dominicano Oregano
- 1 teaspoon of thyme
- ½ to 1 can of tomato paste (6oz)
- 40 oz of vegetable oil *

PRE-PREP

1. Make the sofrito (see page 39).

PREP

1. Cut the vegetables into small pieces.
2. Prepare the Ground Beef Filling:
    a. Partially cook the ground beef, lightly season it, and add ⅓ cup of sofrito to render some fat.
    b. Drain the beef, reserving 1 to 2 tablespoons of fat in the pot. Set the cooked beef aside.
    c. Sauté the vegetables with ⅓ cup of sofrito over medium heat.
    d. Once the vegetables are softened, return the ground beef to the pot and season.
    e. Stir in the tomato paste and additional sofrito, then season to taste.
    f. Reduce the heat and simmer for 10 to 15 minutes.
    Tip: Taste the filling at this stage and adjust the seasoning to your liking.

Scan or click here to watch video

*Depending on the size of the pot, you may not need to use this amount of oil. Use enough so there is about 2-3 inches of oil at the bottom of the pot.

Beef Empanadas (Cont.)

    g. Allow the filling to cool completely before using.
3. Prepare the Dough:
    a. Defrost the empanada shells.

Assemble and Fry

1. Assemble the Empanadas:
   a. Once the shells have defrosted, place them on a flat surface.
   b. Using a spoon, scoop the filling into the center of each shell. Depending on the size of the empanada shells, you can add 2 to 4 spoonfuls.
   c. Fold the shell over the filling to form a half-moon shape. Seal by pinching the edges with your fingers.
   d. Use a fork to crimp the edges, pressing firmly to seal.
   e. At this stage, you can fry the empanadas immediately, refrigerate them, or freeze them.
   Tip: Store uncooked empanadas in a Ziploc bag, using the plastic dividers from the original package to keep them from sticking together.
2. Fry the Empanadas:
   a. Pour oil into a pot and heat over medium-high heat.
   b. Once the oil is hot, carefully place the empanadas in the oil.
   Tip: To know when the oil is ready, run your hand in some water and sprinkle a few droplets of water into the oil. If the oil sizzles, then it is ready. CAUTION: The oil can pop back so be careful.
   c. Working in batches as to not overload the pan, fry the empanadas until golden brown, about 3-5 minutes. Flip and continue to cook until it is golden and crisp on the other side.
   d. Transfer cooked empanadas to a plate lined with paper towels to drain the excess oil.
   e. Serve warm and enjoy.
   Tip: This dish is often paired with a dipping sauce called *mayoketchup* (see page 53).

Fun Fact
The word *empanada* comes from the Spanish verb *empanar*, which means 'to wrap' or 'to coat in bread.'[6]

Chicken Empanadas

INGREDIENTS

- 2 packs of Goya empanada shells
- 4-6 boneless skinless chicken breasts
- 1 cup of sofrito
- 1 medium yellow onion
- 1 medium red onion
- 1 medium green bell pepper
- 1 medium red bell pepper
- ¼ bunch of fresh cilantro
- ¼ bunch of fresh culantro
- 4 cloves of garlic (2 whole, 2 minced)
- 2 medium plum tomatoes, diced
- 1 ½ tablespoons of chicken bouillon
- 3 ½ teaspoons of Adobo
- 1 tablespoon of Badia Sazón Completa
- ½ teaspoon of black pepper
- ½ teaspoon of paprika
- 4 teaspoons of garlic powder
- ½ teaspoon of onion powder
- ½ teaspoon of oregano
- ½ teaspoon of parsley
- ½ teaspoon of Soy Dominicano Oregano
- ½ teaspoon of thyme
- 1 ½ tablespoons of olive oil
- 3 tablespoons of Badia Naranja Agria
- 40 oz of vegetable oil *

PRE-PREP

1. Make the sofrito (see page 39).

PREP

1. Clean and boil the chicken breasts in a pot of water with the following ingredients:
    - ⅛ red onion
    - ⅛ yellow onion
    - ¼ green bell pepper
    - 2 cloves of garlic
    - 2 teaspoons of garlic powder
    - 2 teaspoons of Adobo
    - 2 teaspoons of chicken bouillon
    - 1 tablespoon of sofrito
    - 2 tablespoons of Badia Naranja Agria
    - A few stems of cilantro and culantro

*Depending on the size of the pot, you may not need to use this amount of oil. Use enough so there is about 2-3 inches of oil at the bottom of the pot.

Chicken Empanadas (Cont.)

Tip #1: Depending on the size of the chicken breasts, boiling can take 25–40 minutes.

Tip #2: Save 1–2 cups of the cooking liquid for later use.

2. Cut the vegetables into small pieces.
3. Shred the chicken breast.

   Tip: Shred using two forks or a mixer for best results.
4. Prepare the filling:
   a. Sauté the vegetables with 1½ tablespoons of olive oil.
      - Halfway through cooking, add 2 tablespoons of sofrito.
   b. Once the vegetables are softened, stir in the shredded chicken.
   c. Add additional sofrito, the seasonings, Badia Naranja Agria, and some of the reserved chicken broth.
   d. Reduce the heat and let simmer for 10–15 minutes.

      Tip: Taste at this stage and adjust the seasoning to your liking.
   e. Allow the filling to cool completely before using.
5. Prepare the Dough:
   a. Defrost the empanada shells.

Assemble and Fry

1. Assemble the Empanadas:
   a. Once the shells have defrosted, place them on a flat surface.
   b. Using a spoon, scoop the filling into the center of each shell. Depending on the size of the empanada shells, you can add 2 to 4 spoonfuls.
   c. Fold the shell over the filling to form a half-moon shape. Seal by pinching the edges with your fingers.
   d. Use a fork to crimp the edges, pressing firmly to seal.
   e. At this stage, you can fry the empanadas immediately, refrigerate them, or freeze them.

      Tip: Store uncooked empanadas in a Ziploc bag, using the plastic dividers from the original package to keep them from sticking together.
2. Fry the Empanadas:
   a. Pour oil into a pot and heat over medium-high heat.
   b. Once the oil is hot, carefully place the empanadas in the oil.

      Tip: To know when the oil is ready, run your hand in some water and sprinkle a few droplets of water into the oil. If the oil sizzles, then it is ready. CAUTION: The oil can pop back so be careful.
   c. Working in batches as to not overload the pan, fry the empanadas until golden brown, about 3-5 minutes. Flip and continue to cook until it is golden and crisp on the other side.
   d. Transfer cooked empanadas to a plate lined with paper towels to drain the excess oil.
   e. Serve warm and enjoy.

      Tip: This dish is often paired with a dipping sauce called *mayoketchup* (see page 53).

Scan or click here to watch video

Fun Fact

National Empanada Day is April 8th.[7]

Tuna Empanadas

INGREDIENTS

- 1 pack of Goya empanada shells
- 4 5oz cans of solid white albacore tuna
- 6 tablespoons of epis
- 1 medium yellow onion
- 1 medium red onion
- 1 medium green bell pepper
- 1 medium red bell pepper
- ¼ bunch of cilantro
- 2 cloves of garlic, minced or chopped
- 2 medium plum tomatoes, diced
- 2 spoonfuls of alcaparrado olives, minced
- 1 teaspoon of Old Bay Seasoning
- 1 ¼ teaspoons of Adobo
- 1 ½ teaspoons of Badia Sazón Completa
- ½ teaspoon of black pepper
- ¾ teaspoon of paprika
- 1 ¼ teaspoon of garlic powder
- ½ teaspoon of onion powder
- ½ teaspoon of oregano
- ½ teaspoon of parsley
- ½ teaspoon of Soy Dominicano Oregano
- ½ teaspoon of thyme
- 1 ½ tablespoons of olive oil
- Squeeze of lime juice
- 40 oz of vegetable oil *

PRE-PREP

1. Make the epis (see page 37).

PREP

1. Cut the vegetables into small pieces.
2. Open and drain the canned tuna.
3. Prepare the Tuna Filling:
    a. Sauté the vegetables in 1½ tablespoons of olive oil.
    b. Halfway through cooking, add 2 tablespoons of epis.
    c. Once the vegetables are softened, add the tuna.
        Tip: Use a fork to break the tuna into smaller chunks.

*Depending on the size of the pot, you may not need to use this amount of oil. Use enough so there is about 2-3 inches of oil at the bottom of the pot.

Tuna Empanadas (Cont.)

   d. Stir in additional epis, the seasonings, and a squeeze of lime juice.
   e. Reduce the heat and let simmer for 10–12 minutes.
      Tip: Taste the filling at this stage and adjust the seasoning to your preference.
   f. Allow the filling to cool completely before using.
2. Prepare the Dough:
   a. Defrost the empanada shells.

Assemble and Fry

1. Assemble the Empanadas:
   a. Once the shells have defrosted, place them on a flat surface.
   b. Using a spoon, scoop the filling into the center of each shell. Depending on the size of the empanada shells, you can add 2 to 4 spoonfuls.
   c. Fold the shell over the filling to form a half-moon shape. Seal by pinching the edges with your fingers.
   d. Use a fork to crimp the edges, pressing firmly to seal.
   e. At this stage, you can fry the empanadas immediately, refrigerate them, or freeze them.
      Tip: Store uncooked empanadas in a Ziploc bag, using the plastic dividers from the original package to keep them from sticking together.
2. Fry the Empanadas:
   a. Pour oil into a pot and heat over medium-high heat.
   b. Once the oil is hot, carefully place the empanadas in the oil.
      Tip: To know when the oil is ready, run your hand in some water and sprinkle a few droplets of water into the oil. If the oil sizzles, then it is ready. CAUTION: The oil can pop back so be careful.
   c. Working in batches as to not overload the pan, fry the empanadas until golden brown, about 3-5 minutes. Flip and continue to cook until it is golden and crisp on the other side.
   d. Transfer cooked empanadas to a plate lined with paper towels to drain the excess oil.
   d. Serve warm and enjoy.
      Tip: This dish is often paired with a dipping sauce called *mayoketchup* (see page 53).

Fun Fact
Around the world, many countries have their own unique take on empanadas, often referred to as patties, meat pies, pastels, or pâté kode, among other names.

Epis

INGREDIENTS

- 2 bunches of fresh parsley
- 2 bunches of fresh cilantro
- 2 bunches of fresh scallions
- 1 medium yellow onion
- 1 medium red onion
- 4 sticks of celery
- 1 medium green bell pepper
- 1 medium red bell pepper
- 10 aji dulce peppers
- 2 2-inch chunk of fresh ginger
- 1 head of garlic
- 10 allspice berries
- 4 stems of fresh rosemary
- 4 stems of fresh thyme
- 2 limes, juiced
- ½ teaspoon of salt
- ½ teaspoon of black pepper
- 1 packet of chicken bouillon
- ½ teaspoon of vinegar

PREP

1. Clean and roughly chop all of the vegetables:
    a. Rinse and soak the parsley and cilantro, then rinse the celery.
    b. Cut the peppers open and remove the seeds.
    c. Peel the garlic and ginger.
    d. Cut the onions into quarters or eighths.

ASSEMBLE

1. Blend all the ingredients together.
    Tip: Start with the ingredients that retain the most water, such as onions, peppers, and celery, then add garlic and ginger, followed by parsley, cilantro, and finally the herbs.
2. Add the lime juice and vinegar, then season with salt, pepper, chicken bouillon, and other spices.

STORING

After preparing the epis, transfer it to a container of your choice and store it in the refrigerator or freezer. When refrigerated, it will keep for up to one week; when frozen, it will last for several months.

MARINADES

Fun Fact
Before the use of blenders and food processors, epis was traditionally prepared with a mortar and pestle.[8]

Green Seasoning

INGREDIENTS

- 2 bunches of fresh culantro (shadow beni)
- 2 bunches of fresh scallions
- 1 medium red onion
- 1 medium yellow onion
- 1 medium green bell pepper
- 1 medium red bell pepper
- 6 ají dulce peppers
- 1 head of garlic
- 10 allspice berries
- 4 stems of fresh rosemary
- 4 stems of fresh thyme
- ½ teaspoon of salt
- ½ teaspoon of pepper
- ½ teaspoon of dried or fresh oregano

PREP

1. Clean and roughly chop all of the vegetables:
   a. Rinse and soak the shadow beni and scallions.
   b. Cut the peppers open and remove the seeds.
   c. Peel the garlic.
   d. Cut the onions into quarters or eighths.

ASSEMBLE

1. Blend the ingredients.
   Tip: Start with the ingredients that retain the most water, such as onions and peppers, then add garlic, scallions, culantro, and the herbs.
2. Once all of the ingredients are blended, season with salt, pepper, oregano, and other spices.

STORING

After preparing the green seasoning, transfer it to a container of your choice and store it in the refrigerator or freezer. It will keep for up to one week in the refrigerator or for several months in the freezer.

Fun Fact
This seasoning serves as the base for many Caribbean dishes, including curry chicken and pumpkin soup.

MARINADES

Sofrito

INGREDIENTS

- 2 medium red onions
- 2 medium yellow onions
- 4 medium plum tomatoes
- 10 aji dulce peppers
- 1 medium cubanelle pepper
- 1 medium red bell pepper
- 1 medium green bell pepper
- 2 bunches of fresh cilantro
- 2 bunches of fresh culantro
- 1 to 2 heads of garlic
- ¼ to 1 cup of pitted alcaparrado olives
- ½ teaspoon of salt
- ½ teaspoon of black pepper
- ½ teaspoon of Soy Dominicano Oregano

PREP

1. Clean and roughly chop all of the vegetables:
   a. Rinse and soak the cilantro and culantro.
   b. Open the peppers and remove the seeds.
   c. Remove the skin from the garlic.
   d. Cut the onions into quarters or eighths.

ASSEMBLE

1. Blend the ingredients.
   Tip: Start with the ingredients that retain the most water, such as tomatoes, onions, and peppers, then add garlic, olives, cilantro and culantro.
2. Add salt, black pepper, and Dominican Oregano.

STORING

After preparing your sofrito, transfer it to a container of your choice and store it in the refrigerator or freezer. It will keep for up to one week in the refrigerator or for several months in the freezer.

Fun Fact

The earliest reference to the dish can be found in the 1324 cookbook "Libre de Sent Soví", under the name a "sofregit".[9]

MARINADES

Mac & Cheese

INGREDIENTS

- 1½ lbs. of uncooked elbow noodles
- 4 cups of shredded extra sharp cheddar cheese
- 4 cups of shredded sharp cheddar cheese
- 4 cups of shredded mild cheddar cheese
- 1 block (8 oz) of mild cheddar cheese
- 1 block (8 oz) of sharp cheddar cheese
- 3 cups of milk
- 8 tablespoons of salted butter
- 4 eggs
- ¼ teaspoon of black pepper
- 1 teaspoon of garlic powder
- ¼ teaspoon of paprika
- ½ teaspoon of parsley
- ½ teaspoon of Lawry's Seasoned Salt

PREP

1. Boil the noodles in salted water for 8-10 minutes.
2. Cut the blocks of cheese into small ½ inch cubes.
3. Create the cheese sauce:
    a. Crack and whisk the eggs in a pot or saucepan.
    b. Once the eggs are mixed, add the milk and seasonings.
    c. Turn the stovetop to low and stir occasionally.
    d. Add a cup of each shredded cheese.
    e. Once the cheese has mostly melted, add the butter.
    f. After the butter has melted, the sauce is finished.

ASSEMBLE AND COOK

1. In a pan, combine the cooked noodles, shredded cheese, and block cheese.
    a. Remember to save enough cheese to cover the top of the mac and cheese.
2. Pour in the cheese sauce and mix.
3. Cover the top with a layer of shredded cheese and lightly season it with black pepper, paprika, parsley, and garlic powder.
4. Cover with aluminum foil and bake in the oven for 45 minutes at 350°F (177°C).
5. Remove the foil 20 minutes into the baking so the top can get golden brown.

Scan or click here to watch video

Fun Fact
James Hemings, a former enslaved chef, is credited with introducing mac and cheese to American cuisine.[10]

Macaroni Salad

INGREDIENTS

- 1 lb. of uncooked elbow macaroni
- 4 eggs
- 4-5 oz cans of solid white albacore tuna
- 1 medium green bell pepper
- ½ medium yellow onion
- 2 ½-3 cups of mayonnaise
- ¼ cup of French's yellow mustard
- ¾ teaspoon of black pepper
- 2 teaspoons of garlic powder
- 1 teaspoon of paprika
- ½ teaspoon of oregano
- 1 teaspoon of onion powder
- ¾ teaspoon of dried parsley
- ½ teaspoon of dried thyme
- 1 ½ teaspoons of Old Bay Seasoning
- 1 ½ teaspoons of Lawry's Seasoned Salt
- 1 cup of sweet relish
- 1-2 sticks of celery (optional)

PREP

1. Boil the noodles and eggs.
2. Peel and cut the eggs.
   Tip: Once cooked, place eggs in ice water. After a few seconds, crack the egg underwater and remove the shell.
3. Dice the vegetables.
4. Open, drain, and break up the tuna.

ASSEMBLE

1. Combine the ingredients in the following order:
   - Noodles
   - Tuna
   - Vegetables
   - Eggs
   - Relish
2. Add the other ingredients to season the mix.
3. Incorporate the mayonnaise and mustard, then stir.
   Tip: This is when you should do a taste test and adjust the seasoning to your liking.
4. Chill and serve when ready.

Fun Fact

Like potato salad, macaroni salad is a traditional side dish often prepared for Black American functions, such as cookouts.

PASTA

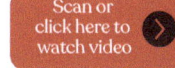

Lasagna

INGREDIENTS
- 16 oz of uncooked lasagna noodles
- 2 ½ lbs. of ground beef
- 1 cup of sofrito
- 1 medium yellow onion
- 1 medium red onion
- 1 medium green bell pepper
- 1 medium red bell pepper
- 3 cloves of garlic, minced
- 14.5 oz of diced tomatoes
- 2 ½ tablespoons of Adobo
- 2 packets of Sazón
- 2 ½ tablespoons of Lawry's Seasoned Salt
- 1 ½ tablespoons of Badia Sazón Completa
- 1 teaspoon of black pepper
- 1 teaspoon of paprika
- 1 tablespoon of garlic powder
- 2 teaspoons of onion powder
- 1½ teaspoon of oregano
- 1½ teaspoon of parsley
- 1 teaspoon of thyme
- ½ can of tomato sauce (29 oz)
- 15 oz of ricotta cheese
- 1 egg
- 4 cups of mozzarella cheese

PRE-PREP
1. Make the sofrito (see page 39).

PREP
1. Chop the vegetables.
2. Prepare the meat sauce:
    a. Partially cook the ground beef, lightly season, and add ⅓ cup of sofrito to release some grease.
    b. Drain the grease, leaving 1–2 tablespoons in the pot.
    c. Set the ground beef aside.
    d. Sauté the vegetables with ⅓ cup of sofrito over medium heat.
    e. Once the vegetables are softened, return the ground beef to the pot and add seasoning.
    f. Stir in the tomato sauce and more sofrito, then season again.
    g. Reduce the heat and simmer for 10–15 minutes.
    h. Taste the filling and adjust the seasoning to your liking.
3. Prepare the noodles:
    a. Boil the lasagna noodles in salted water.
4. Prepare the ricotta mixture:
    a. In a bowl, combine the following ingredients:
        - Ricotta cheese
        - 1 egg
        - ½ teaspoon of black pepper
        - ½ teaspoon of garlic powder
        - ½ teaspoon of parsley
        - ½ teaspoon of oregano
        - ¼ cup of mozzarella cheese

PASTA

Lasagna (Cont.)

ASSEMBLE AND COOK

1. In a baking dish or pan, lightly coat the bottom with meat sauce.
2. Place a layer of lasagna noodles horizontally, then spread the ricotta mixture and sprinkle with cheese.
3. Arrange the next layer of noodles vertically, then add meat sauce and mozzarella cheese on top.
4. Continue layering until you either run out of ingredients or reach your desired number of layers.
5. Finish with a final layer of noodles, topped with cheese and meat sauce. Lightly season.
6. Cover with aluminum foil and bake at 350°F (177°C) for 45 minutes.
7. Halfway through baking, remove the foil to allow the top to brown.
8. Remove from the oven and let rest about 10 minutes before serving.

Fun Fact
Though it is recognized as an Italian dish, lasagna can be traced further back to Ancient Greece. National Lasagna Day is July 29th."

Spaghetti

INGREDIENTS

- 16 oz of uncooked spaghetti noodles
- 24 oz of tomato sauce
- 2 ½ lbs. of ground beef
- 1 pack of Premio Italian sausage links (6 links)
- 1 medium green bell pepper
- 1 medium yellow onion
- 2 cloves of garlic, chopped
- ½ teaspoon of black pepper
- 1 teaspoon of onion powder
- 2 teaspoons of garlic powder
- 1 teaspoon of paprika
- ½ teaspoon of thyme
- ½ teaspoon of oregano
- ½ teaspoon of parsley
- 1 tablespoon of Lawry's Seasoned Salt
- 1 tablespoon of Adobo
- ¼ to ½ cup of water

PREP

1. Dice the onions, peppers, and garlic.
2. Remove the casings from the Italian sausage.
3. Boil the noodles in salted water.
   Tip: Complete this step closer to when the meat sauce is ready.

COOK

1. Combine the ground beef and Italian sausage in a pot and cook.
2. As the meat cooks, lightly season and stir occasionally to prevent burning.
3. Once the meat is about 80% cooked, remove it from the pot. Drain most of the grease, reserving a small amount.
4. Sauté and season the onions, peppers, and garlic in 1 tablespoon of the reserved grease.
5. When the vegetables are softened, return the meat to the pot.
6. Season the mixture and add a bottle of tomato sauce.
   a. To ensure you use all of the sauce, pour ¼–½ cup of water into the bottle, shake, and add it to the pot.
7. Cook on medium-low heat for 10 minutes.
8. Taste and adjust the seasoning as needed.
9. When plating the spaghetti, you can choose one of the following:
   a. Combine the meat sauce and noodles together.
   b. Keep the sauce and noodles separate, drizzling the sauce over the noodles when serving.

Fun Fact

This dish was introduced to African American families in the late 1800s and early 1900s, when Italian immigrants settled in the South.[12]

Chuletas 🇵🇷

INGREDIENTS

- 1 pack of 8 bone-in thin center-cut pork chops
- 1 packet of Sazón
- 2 teaspoons of garlic
- 1 teaspoon of Badia Sazón Completa
- 1 ½ teaspoons of Adobo
- ½ teaspoon of black pepper
- ½ teaspoon of paprika
- ½ teaspoon of oregano
- ½ teaspoon of Soy Dominicano Oregano
- ½ teaspoon of thyme
- 1 teaspoon of Badia Mojo seasoning
- Squeeze of lime juice
- 24 oz of vegetable oil *

PREP

1. Clean the pork chops with water, lime, and vinegar.
2. Season and marinate the pork chops for at least 30 minutes.
3. Pour oil into a large pan.
4. Preheat the pan for a few minutes before frying the pork chops.

COOK

1. Once the oil is hot, add the pork chops and fry until golden brown on both sides.
2. When cooked, transfer the pork chops to a plate lined with paper towels to absorb excess oil.

Fun Fact

This dish pairs perfectly with arroz con gandules, tostones, salad and mayoketchup (see page 53).

*Depending on the size of the pot, you may not need to use this amount of oil. Use enough so there is about 1-3 inches of oil at the bottom of the pot.

Pernil

INGREDIENTS

- 10-12 lb. pork shoulder
- 2 cups of sofrito
- 10 cloves of garlic, chopped
- 10 alcaparrado olives, chopped
- ½ medium red onion
- ½ medium yellow onion
- ½ medium green bell pepper
- ½ medium red bell pepper
- 1 medium tomato
- 3 tablespoons of garlic powder
- 1 tablespoon of onion powder
- 2 packets of Sazón
- 2 tablespoons of Adobo
- 2 tablespoons of Badia Sazón Completa
- 1 teaspoon of black pepper
- 1 teaspoon of paprika
- 1 teaspoon of oregano
- 1 teaspoon of Soy Dominicano Oregano
- 1 teaspoon of parsley
- 1 teaspoon of thyme
- 1 Reynolds Kitchen Oven Bag

PRE-PREP

1. Make the sofrito (see page 39).
2. Clean the pernil:
    a. Trim excess fat from the pork shoulder.
    b. Keeping the skin attached, cut the skin back and poke deep holes all over the pork shoulder.
    c. Cut the limes into quarters and scrub them over the pork shoulder.
    d. Soak the pork in cold water, lime juice, and vinegar for 5–10 minutes.
    e. Rinse and soak one or two additional times.
    f. Drain the water and let the pork rest to remove excess moisture.

PREP

1. Chop the vegetables into small to medium-sized pieces.
2. Once most of the excess water has drained, fill the holes in the pork shoulder with the chopped vegetables.
3. Season the pork shoulder with the listed ingredients.
   Tip: Divide the seasonings in half. Use the first half for the area that will be covered by the skin, and the second half for the bottom and around the bone. Be sure to rub the seasoning into the holes.

PORK

Scan or click here to watch video

Pernil (Cont.)

4. Massage the sofrito into the pernil.
5. Marinate the pernil for anywhere between 2 hours to 3 days.
6. Prepare the oven bag.

COOK

1. When ready to cook, place the pork shoulder in an oven bag.
   a. Important: Follow the instructions provided with the oven bag.
2. Roast the pork shoulder at 350°F (177°C) for 5–6 hours.
3. During the last 2 hours, cut the oven bag open just enough to expose the skin and baste it with the juices to help crisp it.
4. Once the pernil is fully cooked, remove it from the oven and let it rest for 10–15 minutes.
5. Shred the pork and transfer it to another pan.
6. Add 1–3 cups of the juice from the pernil, then serve.

Fun Fact

Pernil can be enjoyed year-round, but in Latin America it is a staple holiday dish, often served with arroz con gandules and pasteles.[13]

Arroz Con Gandules

INGREDIENTS

- 2 cups of uncooked extra-long grain white rice
- 4 cups of water
- 4 tablespoons of sofrito
- 1 15 oz can of gandules (green pigeon peas)
- 1 tablespoon of olive oil
- 1 packet of Sazón
- 1 packet of chicken bouillon
- ½ teaspoon of black pepper
- 2 teaspoons of garlic powder
- 1 teaspoon of dried oregano
- 1 teaspoon of Soy Dominicano Oregano
- 1 teaspoon of thyme
- 2 teaspoons of Badia Sazón Completa
- 1 teaspoon of parsley
- 1 teaspoon of paprika
- ½ teaspoon of onion powder
- 1 tablespoon of tomato paste

PRE-PREP

1. Make the sofrito (see page 39).

PREP

1. Drain the gandules.
2. Wash the rice.

COOK

1. Sauté the sofrito and tomato paste in olive oil over low heat.
2. Season the sofrito and tomato paste.
3. Add the gandules and water to the pot.
4. Increase the heat to medium and mix the ingredients.
5. Taste the broth and adjust the seasoning to your liking.
6. Once the water reaches a boil, add the washed rice.
7. Reduce the heat slightly and stir every 2 minutes.
8. After most of the water has evaporated, sculpt the rice into the shape of a mountain, cover the pot with foil and place the lid on.
9. Lower the heat and cook for 25–30 minutes.
10. Remove the lid, fluff the rice, and serve.

Fun Fact

Arroz con gandules is considered the national dish of Puerto Rico.[14]

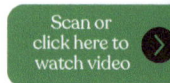

Red Rice

INGREDIENTS

- 12 oz of bacon
- 1 medium green bell pepper
- 1 medium red onion
- 1 medium yellow onion
- 1-6 oz can of tomato paste
- 2 bay leaves
- 2 cups of Uncle Ben's Parboiled Rice, uncooked
- 3½ cups of water or chicken broth
- 1-2 garlic cloves, minced
- 2 teaspoons of Lawry's Seasoned Salt
- ¾ teaspoon of black pepper
- 1½ teaspoons of garlic powder
- ½ teaspoon of dried oregano
- ½ teaspoon of paprika
- ¼ teaspoon of sugar
- ½ teaspoon of vinegar
- 1 packet of chicken bouillon
- 1 tablespoon of bacon grease or olive oil

PREP

1. Cook the bacon and reserve the grease.
2. Chop the bacon into medium-sized pieces.
3. Chop the vegetables.
4. Wash the rice.

COOK

1. On low heat, add bacon grease or olive oil to a pot.
2. Add and sauté the vegetables.
3. Stir in the tomato paste, bacon, and seasonings.
4. Increase the heat to medium and add water.
5. Taste the broth and adjust the seasoning to your liking.
6. Once the water reaches a boil, add the washed rice.
7. Reduce the heat slightly and stir every 2–3 minutes.
8. After most of the water has evaporated, sculpt the rice into the shape of a mountain, cover the pot with foil and place the lid on.
9. Reduce the heat and cook for 20–25 minutes.
10. Remove the lid, fluff the rice, and serve.

Fun Fact
This dish is inspired by Jollof rice, a beloved West African party dish.

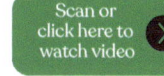 

Rice and Peas

INGREDIENTS

- 2 cups of uncooked extra-long grain white rice
- 1 13.5 oz can of coconut milk
- 2 cups of water
- 3 tablespoons of green seasoning
- 16 oz bag of red kidney beans
- 3 stems of thyme
- 3 cloves of garlic
- 1 1-inch chunk of ginger
- 1 ½ tablespoons of minced ginger
- 3 bay leaves
- 10 allspice berries
- 3 scallions
- 1 tablespoon of olive oil
- 1 packet of chicken bouillon
- ½ teaspoon of black pepper
- 2 teaspoons of garlic powder
- 1 teaspoon of dried oregano
- 1 teaspoon of ginger powder
- 1 teaspoon of thyme
- 1 teaspoon of Blue Mountain Country Garlic, Scallion, Allspice Seasoning
- ¼ teaspoon of salt
- 1 scotch bonnet pepper (optional)

PRE-PREP

1. Make the green seasoning (see page 38).
2. Sort the beans.
   Tip: Beans should be smooth and free of damage. Discard any that are discolored, broken, moldy, or shriveled.
3. Rinse and soak the beans overnight, or for at least 6 hours.

PREP

1. Peel, rinse, and roughly chop the vegetables.
2. In a pot, boil the red kidney beans in water with 1 tablespoon of green seasoning, along with allspice berries, fresh thyme, chunk of ginger and the vegetables for 60–75 minutes.
   Tip: The beans are ready when they are tender and can be easily mashed with a fork.
3. Wash the rice.
   Tip: Complete this step closer to when the beans are done cooking.

Rice and Peas (Cont.)

COOK

1. Once the beans are prepared, remove the cooked chopped vegetables.
2. Add coconut milk, water, minced ginger, the remaining chopped vegetables, and the seasonings.
3. Set the heat to medium and stir the mixture.
4. Taste the broth and adjust the seasoning to your liking.
5. When the broth reaches a boil, add the washed rice.
6. Reduce the heat slightly and stir every 2–3 minutes.
7. Once most of the water has evaporated, cover the pot with foil and place the lid on top.
8. Lower the heat and cook for 25–30 minutes.
9. Remove the lid, fluff the rice, and serve.

Fun Fact

One of the key influences behind rice and peas comes from the Ghanaian dish known as Waakye.

Dominican Potato Salad

INGREDIENTS

- 4 medium yellow potatoes
- 3 eggs
- 2 medium carrots, peeled
- ½ medium green bell pepper
- ½ medium red bell pepper
- ¼ medium red onion
- 1 15 oz can of sliced beets
- 1 ½ to 2 cups of mayonnaise
- ½ teaspoon of black pepper
- 2 teaspoons of garlic powder
- 1 ½ teaspoon of Adobo
- 2 teaspoons of Badia Sazón Completa
- ½ teaspoon of Soy Dominicano Oregano
- ½ teaspoon of paprika
- ½ teaspoon of oregano
- ½ teaspoon of onion powder
- ½ teaspoon of dried parsley
- ½ teaspoon of dried thyme
- 2-3 tablespoons of beet juice
- 1 ½ teaspoons of vinegar from the pickled red onions

PRE-PREP

1. Boil the potatoes and eggs.
2. Peel and boil the carrots.
3. Dice the red onion and submerge it in vinegar.

PREP

1. Peel and cut the potatoes and eggs.
   Tip #1: Once cooked, place the eggs in ice water. After a few seconds, crack them underwater to remove the shells easily.
   Tip #2: Do not peel or cut the potatoes until they have cooled completely.
2. Dice the peppers and carrots.
3. Prepare the beets:
   a. Dice the beets. Save the beet juice for later.

ASSEMBLE

1. In a bowl, combine the ingredients in the following order:
   a. Potatoes
   b. Eggs, beets, and carrots
   c. Peppers, onions, and pickled onion juice
2. Season the potato salad.
3. Add the mayonnaise and stir to combine.
4. Mix in the beet juice and stir until the salad turns pink.
   Tip: Taste and adjust the seasoning to your liking at this stage.
5. Chill before serving.

Fun Fact

The potato salad gets its pink color from the beets and their juices.

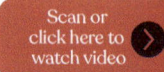

Mayoketchup

INGREDIENTS

- 1 cup of mayonnaise
- 2 ½ tablespoons of ketchup
- 1 ½ teaspoons of vinegar
- 1 teaspoon of garlic powder
- ½ teaspoon of black pepper
- ½ teaspoon of Badia Sazón Completa
- ½ teaspoon of parsley
- ¼ teaspoon of Soy Dominicano Oregano
- ¼ teaspoon of Adobo

ASSEMBLE

1. In a bowl, combine mayonnaise, ketchup, and seasoning.
2. Add vinegar and mix thoroughly.
3. Taste and adjust to your preference.
   Tip: If the sauce is too salty or heavily seasoned, add more mayonnaise. If it's too acidic from the vinegar, add a little sugar.

Fun Fact
This sauce pairs well with dishes such as empanadas, fried plantains, and chimis.

Pastelón

INGREDIENTS

- 4 medium overripe sweet plantains
- 4 cups of mozzarella cheese
- 18 oz of Tropical Queso de Freír (Dominican fried cheese)
- 2 ½ lbs. of ground beef
- 1-2 8 oz cans of Goya tomato sauce
- 2 eggs
- 1 cup of sofrito
- 1 medium yellow onion
- 1 medium red onion
- 1 medium green bell pepper
- 1 medium red bell pepper
- ¼ bunch of fresh cilantro
- ¼ bunch of fresh culantro
- 3 cloves of garlic, minced or chopped
- 2 medium plum tomatoes, diced
- 2 ½ tablespoons of Adobo
- 2 packets of Sazón
- 2 ½ tablespoons of Badia Sazón Completa
- 1 teaspoon of black pepper
- 1 teaspoon of paprika
- 1 tablespoon of garlic powder
- 2 teaspoons of onion powder
- 1 teaspoon of oregano
- 1 teaspoon of parsley
- 1 tablespoon of Soy Dominicano Oregano
- 1 teaspoon of thyme
- 24 oz vegetable oil *

PRE-PREP

1. Make the sofrito (see page 39).

PREP

1. Chop the vegetables.
2. Cut the queso de freír into thin horizontal strips.
3. Prepare the meat filling:
    a. Partially cook the ground beef, lightly season it, and add ⅓ cup of sofrito to release some grease.
    b. Drain the grease, leaving 1 to 2 tablespoons in the pot.
    c. Set the ground beef aside.
    d. Sauté the vegetables with one-third of the sofrito over medium heat.

*Depending on the size of the pot, you may not need to use this amount of oil. Use enough so there is about ¼ - ½ inch of oil at the bottom of the pot.

Pastelón (Cont.)

    e. Return the ground beef to the pot and add seasoning.
    f. Stir in tomato sauce and more sofrito, then season again.
    g. Reduce the heat and let the mixture simmer for 10–15 minutes.
    h. Taste the filling and adjust the seasoning as desired.
4. Cut the sweet plantains into vertical strips and fry in vegetable oil until golden.
5. Crack the eggs into a bowl and whisk until blended.

ASSEMBLE AND COOK

1. In a baking dish or pan, lightly coat the bottom with a layer of meat filling.
2. Arrange the sweet plantains vertically and brush with a thin layer of egg.
3. Add a layer of meat and mozzarella cheese.
4. Top with another layer of sweet plantain and egg, followed by a layer of queso de freír.
5. Continue layering until you run out of ingredients or reach your desired thickness.
6. Finish with a final layer of plantain, then top with cheese and meat sauce and add some garlic powder, black pepper, and dried parsley to the top for some added color.
7. Cover with aluminum foil and bake at 350°F (177°C) for 45 minutes.
    a. Halfway through baking, remove the foil to allow the top to brown.
8. Remove from the oven and serve warm.

Scan or click here to watch video

Fun Fact
Rumor has it this dish originated in New York City in the mid-1900s, created by Puerto Rican and Dominican Americans, and was likely inspired by Italian lasagna.[15]

Red Onions

INGREDIENTS

- 1 large red onion
- ½ cup of vinegar
- ½ teaspoon garlic powder
- ¼ teaspoon Adobo
- ½ teaspoon Badia Sazón Completa
- ¼ teaspoon Soy Dominicano Oregano
- ½-1 cup of water
- 2-3 tablespoons of olive oil

PREP

1. Slice the onions into rings and separate the layers.

COOK

1. Heat a pan and add olive oil.
2. Add the onions and cook over low heat, stirring occasionally, until translucent.
3. Season the onions, then stir in the vinegar and continue cooking gently.
4. Gradually add the water, then remove from the heat.
5. Once cooled, transfer the onions to a container and refrigerate. Chilling enhances their crisp texture.

Fun Fact
Red onions pair beautifully with roasted or stewed meats and complement rice dishes as well.

Candy Yams

INGREDIENTS
- 3 large sweet potatoes
- 8 tablespoons of salted butter
- 1 cup of sugar
- ½ cup of brown sugar
- ½ teaspoon of cinnamon
- ½ teaspoon of nutmeg
- ½ teaspoon of ground allspice
- ½ teaspoon of ground clove
- Squeeze of lemon juice
- ½ cup of water

PREP
1. Wash, peel, and chop the sweet potatoes.

COOK
1. Place all ingredients in a pot and set the stove to low–medium heat.
2. Cook the yams for about 20 minutes, or until softened (cooking time may vary depending on thickness of the potatoes).

Bake
1. Transfer the yams to a baking pan and bake at 350°F (177°C) for 30 minutes, or until golden brown.

Fun Fact
Sweet potatoes were introduced to enslaved people as a substitute for yams, which did not grow well in the United States.[16]

Caldeirada de Cabrito

INGREDIENTS

- 3 lbs. of cut up goat
- 8 oz chorizo sausage (1 link)
- 1 medium yellow onion
- 1 medium red bell pepper
- 1 medium green bell pepper
- 2 medium carrots, peeled
- 2 garlic cloves, minced
- ¼ cup of black olives
- ¼ cup of green olives
- 3 medium yellow potatoes
- 2 packets of chicken bouillon
- 2 cups of white cooking wine
- 4 teaspoons of pepper soup mix or:
    - 2 teaspoons of nutmeg
    - 2 teaspoons of cinnamon
    - 1 teaspoon of ground clove
    - 2 teaspoons of ground allspice
    - 2 teaspoons of ginger powder
    - 3 teaspoons of garlic powder
- 4 teaspoons of garlic powder
- 1 teaspoon of black pepper
- 1 teaspoon of paprika
- 1 teaspoon of onion powder
- 1 teaspoon of white pepper
- ½ teaspoon of oregano
- ½ teaspoon of parsley
- ½ teaspoon of thyme
- ½ teaspoon of salt
- 1 ½ tablespoons of olive oil

PRE-PREP

1. If not already prepared, combine the ingredients to the pepper soup seasoning mix.
2. Clean the goat meat:
    - Remove any excess fat.
    - Soak in cold water with lime and vinegar.

Caldeirada de Cabrito (Cont.)

PREP

3. Season and marinate the meat for at least 1 hour.
    - Marinade:
        - 1 packet of chicken bouillon
        - ½ cup of white cooking wine
        - 2 teaspoons of pepper soup mix
        - 2 teaspoons of garlic powder
        - ½ teaspoon of black pepper
        - ½ teaspoon of paprika
        - ½ teaspoon of onion powder
        - ½ teaspoon of white pepper
        - ¼ teaspoon of salt
    - After seasoning the goat, add bay leaves and some of the onions, then marinate together.
4. Prepare the remaining ingredients:
    - Cut the chorizo.
    - Chop the vegetables.
    - Open and drain the olives.

COOK

1. In a pot with olive oil, sear the marinated goat meat.
2. Add enough water to cover the meat and cook until tender. As the water reduces, replenish it once or twice to ensure the meat cooks through.
3. When the meat is tender and most of the water has reduced, add the garlic and chorizo and cook them.
4. Add more water, along with the remaining seasoning, cooking wine, vegetables, and potatoes.
5. Simmer over low to medium heat for 20–25 minutes.
   Tip #1: Skim off any grease that rises to the edges while cooking.
   Tip #2: The soup is ready when the potatoes are fork-tender.
6. Taste the broth and adjust the seasoning to your liking.
7. Turn off the heat and serve.

Fun Fact

Caldeirada de Cabrito, or goat stew, is a traditional dish often prepared in honor of Angola's Independence Day on November 11.[17]

Chicken Noodle Soup

INGREDIENTS

- 5 chicken drumsticks
- 5 chicken thighs
- 12 oz of egg noodles
- 1 medium yellow onion
- 1 medium green bell pepper
- 2 sticks of celery
- 3 medium carrots, peeled
- 2 garlic cloves, minced
- 1½ cup of epis
- 4 teaspoons of garlic powder
- 1½ teaspoons of Badia Sazón Completa
- 1½ teaspoons of turmeric
- 1½ teaspoons of ginger powder
- 1 teaspoon of oregano
- 1 teaspoon of paprika
- 1 teaspoon of thyme
- 1 teaspoon of parsley
- 1 teaspoon of black pepper
- 2 teaspoons of Adobo
- 2 teaspoons of Blue Mountain Country Garlic, Scallion, Allspice Seasoning
- 2 packets of chicken bouillon
- 2 bay leaves
- 32 oz of chicken broth
- 4 cups of water
- 1½ tablespoons of olive oil
- 2 capfuls of vinegar

PRE-PREP

1. Make the epis (see page 37).

PREP

1. Clean the chicken:
    a. Remove the skin and excess fat.
    b. Soak in cold water with lime and vinegar.
2. Season and marinate for at least 30 minutes.
    a. Marinade:
        - 3 tablespoons of epis
        - 1 ½ teaspoons of garlic powder
        - 1 teaspoon of Badia Sazón Completa
        - 1 teaspoon of turmeric
        - 1 teaspoon of ginger powder
        - ½ teaspoon of oregano

Chicken Noodle Soup (Cont.)

- ½ teaspoon of oregano
- ½ teaspoon of paprika
- ½ teaspoon of thyme
- ½ teaspoon of parsley
- ½ teaspoon of black pepper
- 1 teaspoon of Adobo
- 1 teaspoon of Blue Mountain Country Garlic, Scallion, Allspice Seasoning
- 1 packet of chicken bouillon

3. Chop the vegetables.
4. Boil the egg noodles in a separate pot and set them aside.
   Tip: Do this step while the chicken is simmering.

COOK

1. Brown the chicken in a pot, then remove and set aside.
2. Add olive oil to the pot, followed by the vegetables and epis, and sauté until softened.
3. Return the chicken to the pot and season.
4. Pour in 1 box of chicken broth along with water.
5. Add additional seasoning, vinegar, bay leaves, and epis.
6. Simmer the soup over low to medium heat for 20–25 minutes.
   Tip: The soup is ready when the chicken falls off the bone. Feel free to also shred the chicken with a fork.
7. Taste the broth and adjust the seasoning to your liking.
8. Stir in the pre-boiled noodles and serve.

Fun Fact
Chicken noodle soup dates back to ancient civilizations as early as 6000 BC, with evidence suggesting it was often consumed as a remedy for illness.[18]

Sancocho

INGREDIENTS

- 5 chicken thighs
- 5 chicken drumsticks
- 2-3 lbs. of beef stew
- 2 lbs. of thin cut pork tenderloin
- 3-4 cups of 1-inch chunks of calabaza pumpkin
- 3 medium carrots, peeled
- 4 ears of corn
- 2 medium plum tomatoes
- 1 medium malanga or yautia
- 2 medium yucca roots
- 2 large green plantains
- 2 cups of sofrito
- 1 medium red onion
- 1 medium yellow onion
- 1 medium green bell pepper
- 1 medium red bell pepper
- 3 garlic cloves, minced
- ¼ bunch of fresh cilantro
- ¼ bunch of fresh culantro
- 2 packets of chicken bouillon
- 1 beef bouillon cube
- 4-5 teaspoons of Adobo
- 4-5 teaspoons of Badia Sazón Completa
- 2 teaspoons of black pepper
- 2 teaspoons of paprika
- 4-5 teaspoons of garlic powder
- 2 teaspoons of onion powder
- 2 teaspoons of oregano
- 2 teaspoons of parsley
- 2 teaspoons of Soy Dominicano Oregano
- 2 teaspoons of thyme
- 3 teaspoons of Ranchero Salsa Inglesa
- 2 tablespoons of Badia Naranja Agria
- 2 bay leaves
- 1 capful of vinegar

PRE-PREP

1. Prepare the sofrito (see page 39).
2. Clean the meat:
    a. Remove any skin and excess fat.
    b. Soak in cold water with lime and vinegar.
    c. Season and marinate for at least 1 hour. (Marinade ingredients listed on next page.)

Sancocho (Cont.)

Marinade Measurements:

<u>Chicken</u>

- 1 packet of chicken bouillon
- 2 tablespoons of sofrito
- 1 teaspoon of Adobo
- 1 teaspoon of Badia Sazón Completa
- ½ teaspoon of black pepper
- ½ teaspoon of paprika
- 1 teaspoon of garlic powder
- ½ teaspoon of onion powder
- ½ teaspoon of oregano
- ½ teaspoon of parsley
- ½ teaspoon of thyme
- 1 teaspoon of Ranchero Salsa
- ½ teaspoon of Soy Dominicano Oregano

<u>Beef</u>

- 1 packet of Sazón
- 2 tablespoons of sofrito
- 1 teaspoon of Adobo
- 1 teaspoon of Badia Sazón Completa
- ½ teaspoon of black pepper
- ½ teaspoon of paprika
- 1 teaspoon of garlic powder
- ½ teaspoon of onion powder
- ½ teaspoon of oregano
- ½ teaspoon of parsley
- ½ teaspoon of thyme
- 1 tablespoon of Badia Naranja Agria
- 1 teaspoon of Ranchero Salsa Inglesa
- ½ teaspoon of Soy Dominicano Oregano

<u>Pork</u>

- 1 tablespoon of Badia Naranja Agria
- 2 tablespoons of sofrito
- 1 teaspoon of Adobo
- 1 teaspoon of Badia Sazón Completa
- ½ teaspoon of black pepper
- ½ teaspoon of paprika
- 1 teaspoon of garlic powder
- ½ teaspoon of onion powder
- ½ teaspoon of oregano
- ½ teaspoon of parsley
- ½ teaspoon of thyme
- 1 teaspoon of Ranchero Salsa
- ½ teaspoon of Soy Dominicano Oregano
- 1 tablespoon of Badia Mojo seasoning

PREP

1. Chop the vegetables, dicing half and cutting the other half into vertical strips.
2. Peel and chop the root vegetables and starches.
   Tip: Cut root vegetables into medium to large size chunks.

COOK

1. In a pot, combine olive oil and brown sugar. Then, add the chicken and remove it once it's browned on both sides.
2. Add a little more olive oil, then sauté half of the onions, peppers, garlic, and sofrito.
3. After the vegetables are softened, add the beef.
4. Pour in the chicken broth along with water, and cook for 10–20 minutes.
5. Halfway through, return the chicken to the pot.
6. Add additional seasoning, vinegar, bay leaves, and more sofrito.
7. Once the soup comes to a boil, add the pork.
8. When the soup reaches a boil again, skim off any grease from the surface, then add the yuca, plantains, and other root vegetables.
9. At the third boil, add the remaining vegetables and seasonings.
   Tip: To thicken the stew, mash a few pieces of pumpkin, yuca, and plantain with some broth, then stir them back into the soup.
10. Simmer over low to medium heat for 15–25 minutes.
    Tip: The soup is ready when the yuca, plantains, and other root vegetables are fork-tender.
11. Taste the broth and adjust the seasoning as needed.
12. Turn off the heat and serve with white rice and lime.

<u>Fun Fact</u>

Sancocho reflects influences from African, Native American, and European cuisines. Its name comes from the Spanish word *sancochar*, meaning "to parboil".[19]

Banana Bread

INGREDIENTS

- 3 medium ripe bananas
- 8 tablespoons of salted butter, melted
- 1 tablespoon of vanilla
- ½ teaspoon of cinnamon
- ¼ teaspoon of nutmeg
- ¼ teaspoon of allspice
- ¼ teaspoon of clove
- 2 eggs
- ½ cup of milk
- ¾ cup of sugar
- ½ cup of brown sugar
- 1 teaspoon of baking powder
- 1 teaspoon of baking soda
- 1 ½ cups of all-purpose flour
- Pam baking spray

PREP

1. In a pan, melt the butter over low heat.
2. In a bowl, mash the ripe bananas until smooth.
3. Prepare the batter by combining the wet ingredients together.
4. Add the dry ingredients to the same bowl.
5. Stir in the melted butter until fully incorporated.

BAKE

1. Coat the baking pan with the Pam baking spray.
2. Pour the batter into the pan and bake at 350°F (177°C) for 45–50 minutes, or until a toothpick inserted in the center comes out clean.
3. Allow to cool before serving.

Fun Fact
This dish originated during the Great Depression.[20]

Pudin De Pan

INGREDIENTS
- 1 20 oz loaf of preferred bread
- 1 12 oz can of evaporated milk
- 1 13.5 oz can of coconut milk
- 1 cup of sugar
- ½ cup of brown sugar
- 1 tablespoon of vanilla
- ½ teaspoon of cinnamon
- ½ teaspoon of nutmeg
- ¼ teaspoon of ground allspice
- ¼ teaspoon of ground cloves
- 4 eggs
- 8 tablespoons of salted butter, melted
- 1-2 cups of milk
- Pam Baking Spray

Optional Ingredients
- ½ cup of Coco Lopez Crema de Coco
- ¼ cup of coconut flakes
- 1 oz of Craisins or raisins

PREP
1. Tear the bread into small pieces and place them in a large bowl.
   - If using Craisins, raisins or coconut flakes, add them to the bowl with the bread.
2. In a separate bowl, whisk together the eggs, milk, sugar, and spices.
   - If adding Crèma de Coco, include it in the liquid mixture.
3. Melt the butter over low heat.
4. Pour the liquid mixture over the bread and let it soak for 2–4 minutes, then stir to combine.
5. Once the batter is fully mixed, add the melted butter and stir until it is completely incorporated.

BAKE
1. Lightly coat the baking dish with nonstick baking spray.
2. Pour the mixture into the dish and bake at 350°F (177°C) for 50–60 minutes, or until golden.
3. Once removed from the oven, let it set for at least 1 hour and serve.

Fun Fact
In the 13th century, this dessert was known as "poor man's pudding." It was later brought to the New World by the English during colonization.[21]

Sweet Potato Pie

INGREDIENTS

- Pie crust
- 2 medium-large sweet potatoes
- 2 eggs
- 1 tablespoon of vanilla
- 1 cup of sugar
- ½ cup of brown sugar
- ½ teaspoon of cinnamon
- ¼ teaspoon of nutmeg
- ¼ teaspoon of ground allspice
- ¼ teaspoon of ground clove
- 4 tablespoons of salted butter, melted
- Squeeze of lemon juice
- 1-2 cups of evaporated milk

PRE-PREP

1. When cooking sweet potatoes, you have two options. You can either:
    a. Roast sweet potatoes in the oven at 400°F (204°C) until tender.
        - Rinse off the sweet potatoes.
        - Use a fork to poke holes into the sweet potatoes.
        - Wrap the potatoes in aluminum foil, place them on a baking sheet, and bake until tender.
    b. Boil the sweet potatoes:
        - Rinse off and poke holes into the potatoes using a fork.
        - Put potatoes in a pot of boiling water and cook until they are fork-tender.

PREP

1. Once the potatoes cool, remove the skin and place them in a bowl.
2. Melt the butter over low heat.
3. Mash the potatoes using a potato masher or a fork.
4. Add vanilla, sugar, spices, milk, butter and lemon juice.
    a. Here is where you can taste the mixture and adjust the flavor to your liking.

Tip: If you want your pie a tad sweeter, add ¼ cup of condensed milk.

 Scan or click here to watch video

Sweet Potato Pie (Cont.)

5. Add the eggs and continue using a whisk and then switch to either a hand-held blender or a regular blender.
6. Prepare the crust as some crusts require them to be baked prior to use.
   Note: Bake time and temperature should be according to the instructions provided by the pie crust.
6. Pour the filling into the prepared crust, smoothing the top evenly.

BAKE

1. Bake at 350°F (177°C) for 45–60 minutes, or until set.
2. Once the pie has finished baking, allow it to cool completely.
3. Cover with aluminum foil and let it rest for at least 6 hours before serving.

Fun Fact
This dessert traces its roots to the cultivation of sweet potatoes by enslaved African Americans, combined with European baking traditions later adopted and adapted by Black families.[22]

Cabbage

INGREDIENTS

- 1 medium-sized head of cabbage
- 1 medium green bell pepper
- 1 medium yellow onion
- 3 medium carrots, peeled
- 3 cloves of garlic, chopped
- ½ teaspoon of black pepper
- 2 ½ teaspoons of garlic powder
- 2 teaspoons of paprika
- 2 teaspoons of onion powder
- 1 pack of chicken bouillon
- 1 teaspoon of vinegar
- ½ cup of water
- 1 tablespoon of olive oil
- 2 teaspoons of Lawry's Seasoned Salt
- Okra (optional)
- 2 lbs. of smoked turkey or pork necks (optional)

PRE-PREP (Optional: If adding smoked meat)

1. Prepare the smoked meat by rinsing it and placing it in a pot of boiling water.
Tip: Simmer for 30 to 45 minutes while you prepare the other ingredients. This will ensure the meat is tender enough to fall off the bone by the time the cabbage is ready.

PREP

1. Chop the cabbage to your preferred size and wash thoroughly.
2. Prepare the other vegetables by cutting them to your desired size.

COOK

1. Once everything is prepared, follow one of the steps below:
   a. With smoked meat: Reserve the water used to boil the meat and set it aside. Heat oil in the pot, then add half of the vegetables along with the meat and sauté.
   b. Without smoked meat: Heat oil in the pot, then add half of the vegetables and sauté.
2. Once the vegetables are translucent, lightly season them and add the water.
   Tip: If using smoked meat, substitute with the reserved cooking liquid.

VEGETABLES

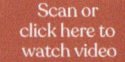

Cabbage (Cont.)

3. Gradually add the cabbage to the pot, covering it after each addition. Continue adding more every 2–3 minutes until all of the cabbage is in the pot.
   Tip: After adding the cabbage, mix it to keep the cooked cabbage on top and the raw cabbage on the bottom.
4. About halfway through cooking, add the remaining seasoning and vinegar. Reduce the heat and simmer for another 10–15 minutes.
   Tip: This is the perfect time to taste and adjust the seasoning to your liking.

Fun Fact
The word cabbage comes from the Latin *caput*, meaning "head".[23]

Collard Greens

INGREDIENTS

- 4 bunches of collard greens
- 3 lbs. of smoked turkey or pork necks
- 1 medium yellow onion
- 1 medium green bell pepper
- 1 medium red bell pepper
- 3 cloves of garlic
- 3 tablespoons of garlic powder
- 2 tablespoons of onion powder
- 32 oz of chicken broth
- 2 tablespoons of paprika
- 2 ½ tablespoons of Lawry's Seasoned Salt
- 1 teaspoon of black pepper
- 1 ½ packets of chicken bouillon
- ¾ teaspoon of crushed red peppers
- 1 ½ teaspoon of vinegar
- 2-3 cups of water

PRE-PREP

1. Cut the vegetables.
2. Prepare the greens:
   a. Using your hands or a knife, remove the leaves from the stems, then chop the collard greens to your preferred size.
   b. Wash thoroughly.

   Tip: Soak the collard greens in cold water with a little salt and vinegar. Swish them around to loosen any dirt, then drain. Repeat this process three more times, or until the water runs clear.

PREP

1. Prepare the smoked meat.
   a. In a little olive oil, sauté and season some of the onions, peppers, and garlic.
   b. Rinse the meat and place it in the pot.
   c. Lightly season the smoked meat and vegetables, then add enough water to fully cover them.

   Tip: Simmer for 30-45 minutes before adding the collard greens. This will ensure the meat is tender enough to fall off the bone by the time the greens are ready.

Collard Greens (Cont.)

COOK

1. After precooking the smoked meat, add the remaining vegetables, chicken broth, seasonings, and water.
2. Once the liquid comes to a boil, begin adding the greens to the pot.
3. Gradually add them in batches, covering the pot each time. Continue this process every 2–3 minutes until all of the greens have been added to the pot.

   Tip: Stir as you go to bring the cooked greens to the top and push the raw greens to the bottom.
4. Once all the greens are added, stir in the remaining seasonings and vinegar. Reduce the heat slightly and simmer for another 30–45 minutes.

   Tip: This is the best time to taste and adjust the seasoning to your liking.

VEGAN/VEGETARIAN ALTERNATIVE

For a meat-free version, omit the smoked meat and substitute the chicken broth with water or vegetable broth.

Fun Fact

Collard greens were among the first vegetable crops that enslaved people in America could harvest and eat for themselves.[24]

Shucked Corn

INGREDIENTS

- 5 ears of corn
- 1 medium green bell pepper
- 1 small yellow onion
- 1 small red onion
- 2 teaspoons of Lawry's Seasoned Salt
- 1 ½ teaspoons of garlic powder
- 1 teaspoon of black pepper
- 1 teaspoon of paprika
- ½ teaspoon of onion powder
- 2 tablespoons of bacon grease or olive oil
- 12 oz of bacon (optional)

PRE-PREP

1. Cook a package of bacon and reserve the rendered grease in a glass jar or heat-safe container.

Note: If you prefer not to use meat, simply skip this step.

PREP

1. Remove the husks and silk from the corn, then rinse.
2. Shuck the corn by cutting the kernels off the cob.
3. Dice the onions and peppers, and chop the bacon into medium-sized pieces.

COOK

1. Heat the bacon grease or olive oil in a pot.
2. Add the chopped vegetables and sauté until the onions and peppers have softened.
3. Stir in the corn and cook gently on low heat for 10–12 minutes, seasoning to taste. Once the corn is tender, fold in the chopped bacon and serve.

Fun Fact
The dish takes its name from the word "shucking," which refers to removing the husk and silk from the corn.

INDEX

ANGOLA
Caldeirada de Cabrito, 58

BERMUDA
Rum Swizzle, 30

BLACK AMERICAN
Banana Bread, 64
Black Eyed Peas, 16
Cabbage, 68
Candy Yams, 57
Chicken Noodle Soup, 60
Chilli, 20
Collard Greens, 70
Fried Chicken, 24
Lasagna, 42
Mac and Cheese, 40
Macaroni Salad, 41
Pudin de Pan, 65
Red Rice, 49
Shucked Corn, 72
Spaghetti, 44
Sweet Potato Pie, 66

CAPE VERDE
Tuna Empanada, 35

CUBA
Pernil, 46

COLOMBIA
Sancocho, 62

DOMINICAN REPUBLIC
Beef Empanada, 31
Beef Stew, 18
Black Beans, 15
Chicken Empanada, 33
Dominican Potato Salad, 52
Habichuela Guisada, 17
Mayoketchup, 53
Morir Soñando, 29
Pernil, 46
Pastelón, 54
Red Onions, 56
Sancocho, 62
Sofrito, 39

HAITI
Chicken Noodle Soup, 60
Epis, 37
Haitian Fried Chicken, 26
Tuna Empanada, 35

JAMAICA
Curry Chicken, 22
Green Seasoning, 38
Rice and Peas, 50

PUERTO RICO
Arroz Con Gandules, 48
Beef Empanada, 31
Chicken Empanada, 33
Chuletas, 45
Coquito, 27
Mayoketchup, 53
Pastelón, 54
Pernil, 46
Pudin de Pan, 65
Sancocho, 62
Sofrito, 39

TRINIDAD
Green Seasoning, 38

USA
Banana Bread, 64

REFERENCES

[2] Abreu, Sami. "Nuestra Latinidad: An Habichuelas Tour of Latin America." *Loisa*, 9 Oct. 2021, loisa.com/blogs/comida-real/nuestra-latinidad-an-habichuelas-tour-of-latin-america.

[21] Allrecipes. "What Is Bread Pudding — and What Kind of Bread Should You Use?" *Allrecipes*, 2023, www.allrecipes.com/article/what-is-bread-pudding/.

[23] "Cabbage." *FoodPrint*, foodprint.org/real-food/cabbage/.

[7] Calendar, National Day. "NATIONAL EMPANADA DAY - April 8." *National Day Calendar*, 31 Mar. 2014, www.nationaldaycalendar.com/national-day/national-empanada-day-april-8. Accessed 17 May 2025.

[14] Caviness, Kim. "The History of Arroz Con Gandules — Plus: 5 Pigeon Peas & Rice Recipes! – Familia Kitchen." *Familia Kitchen*, 17 Nov. 2024, familiakitchen.com/history-of-arroz-con-gandules-plus-5-pigeon-peas-rice-recipes/.

[5] cdickinson. "Tales of Rum Swizzle & the Queen of Bermuda Bermuda.com." *Bermuda.com*, Dec. 2023, www.bermuda.com/tales-of-rum-swizzle-the-queen-of-bermuda/. Accessed 17 May 2025.

[16] Cummings-Yeates, Rosalind. "Confusion and Connection: The Yams and Sweet Potatoes of the African Diaspora." *The Takeout*, The Takeout, 25 June 2021, www.thetakeout.com/yams-vs-sweet-potatoes-history-african-diaspora-1847160775/.

[6] Despres, Marianne. "A Brief History of Empanadas." *El Sur*, 21 Oct. 2024, elsursf.com/blogs/news/a-brief-history-of-empanadas.

[3] Ephanov, Nikita. The History of Beef Stew Can Be Traced Back to 14th Century France." *Yahoo Life*, 4 May 2024.

[15] Ephanov, Nikita. "Pastelón Is the Puerto Rican Plantain Casserole You Should Know." *Tasting Table*, 20 Sept. 2023, www.tastingtable.com/1395383/pastelon-puerto-rican-plantain-casserole-explained/. Accessed 17 May 2025.

[10] Guardian staff reporter. "Why the Black American Origins of Mac and Cheese Are so Hotly Debated." *The Guardian*, The Guardian, 22 Dec. 2024, www.theguardian.com/culture/2024/dec/22/mac-cheese-black-americans.

[18] https://www.facebook.com/Health. "The Science behind Why Chicken Soup Might Make You Feel Better When You're Sick." *Health*, 2024, www.health.com/chicken-soup-health-benefits-8422812.

[24] Kelley, Susan. "Seeds of Survival: Botanic Gardens Honors the Black Experience | Department of Sociology." Cornell.edu, 17 Aug. 2022, sociology.cornell.edu/news/seeds-survival-botanic-gardens-honors-black-experience.

[8] Long, Lucy M. Ethnic American Food Today : A Cultural Encyclopedia. Lanham, Maryland, Rowman & Littlefield, 2015, p. 257.

[17] Mike Stead and Sean Rorison. Angola (2010). Bradt Travel Guides, pp. 81–83.

[12] Miller, Adrian. "Is Fried Fish and Spaghetti Soul Food's Most Debatable Dish?" Heated, 8 Aug. 2019, heated.medium.com/is-fried-fish-and-spaghetti-soul-foods-most-debatable-dish-3ff2c328a311.

[20] Monaco, Emily. "History Behind Banana Bread." Yahoo Life, 16 Sept. 2023.

[11] "National Lasagna Day." Days of the Year, 17 Jan. 2025, www.daysoftheyear.com/days/lasagna-day/.

[19] Payne, Laura. "Sancocho | Description, History, Types, National Dish, & Facts | Britannica." Encyclopædia Britannica, 2024, www.britannica.com/topic/sancocho.

[13] "Puerto Rico's National Dish of Pernil – OBSCURA." CUNY Academic Commons, 7 May 2021, obscura.commons.gc.cuny.edu/2021/05/07/puerto-ricos-national-dish-of-pernil/.

[9] Rodriguez, Hector. "All about Sofrito and How to Use It in Caribbean Cooking." The Spruce Eats, 20 Dec. 2022.

[1] Sandborn, Dixie. "Black Beans and the Science behind Them." 4-H Plants, Soils & Gardening, 1 Dec. 2021, www.canr.msu.edu/news/black_beans_and_the_science_behind_them.

[22] Shepard, Ryan. "For Many African-Americans, Sweet Potato Pie Isn't Just a Dessert, It's about Family." Southern Kitchen, 25 July 2021, www.southernkitchen.com/story/eat/2021/07/25/african-american-history-sweet-potato-pie/8089134002/.

[4] Stewart, Kayla. "Fried Chicken Isn't a Punchline—It's Part of the Black American Story." Life & Thyme, 25 July 2022, lifeandthyme.com/food/fried-chicken-isnt-a-punchline-its-part-of-the-black-american-story/.

DONOVAN TINSLEY
THE MAN BEHIND THE CAMERA

Donovan Tinsley, owner of Soul de Alma, was born and raised in Harlem, New York City. His love for cooking was sparked by watching his parents, family, and church members prepare food for gatherings. These experiences taught him that food was a key component to creating and fostering community.

While competing in speech tournaments, singing in the choir, and participating in church plays, Donovan discovered his passion for the performing arts. This led him to attend Talent Unlimited High School, where he studied theatre. In his junior year, he developed an interest in marketing, which took him to the State of Rhode Island to attend Johnson & Wales University. There, he earned a bachelor's degree in Advertising and Marketing Communications.

While living in Rhode Island, Donovan combined his love for cooking and humor to build community and forge lifelong friendships far from home. In 2023, Soul de Alma was officially born, evolving from a mere idea in 2012 into a vibrant blend of all his favorite passions.

Join Donovan as he continues this empowering journey of self-love, cultural celebration, and culinary exploration.

> "Let food be our gateway to something extraordinary,
> as food serves as the foundation of the empire we are building together."
> - Donovan Tinsley